I0814796

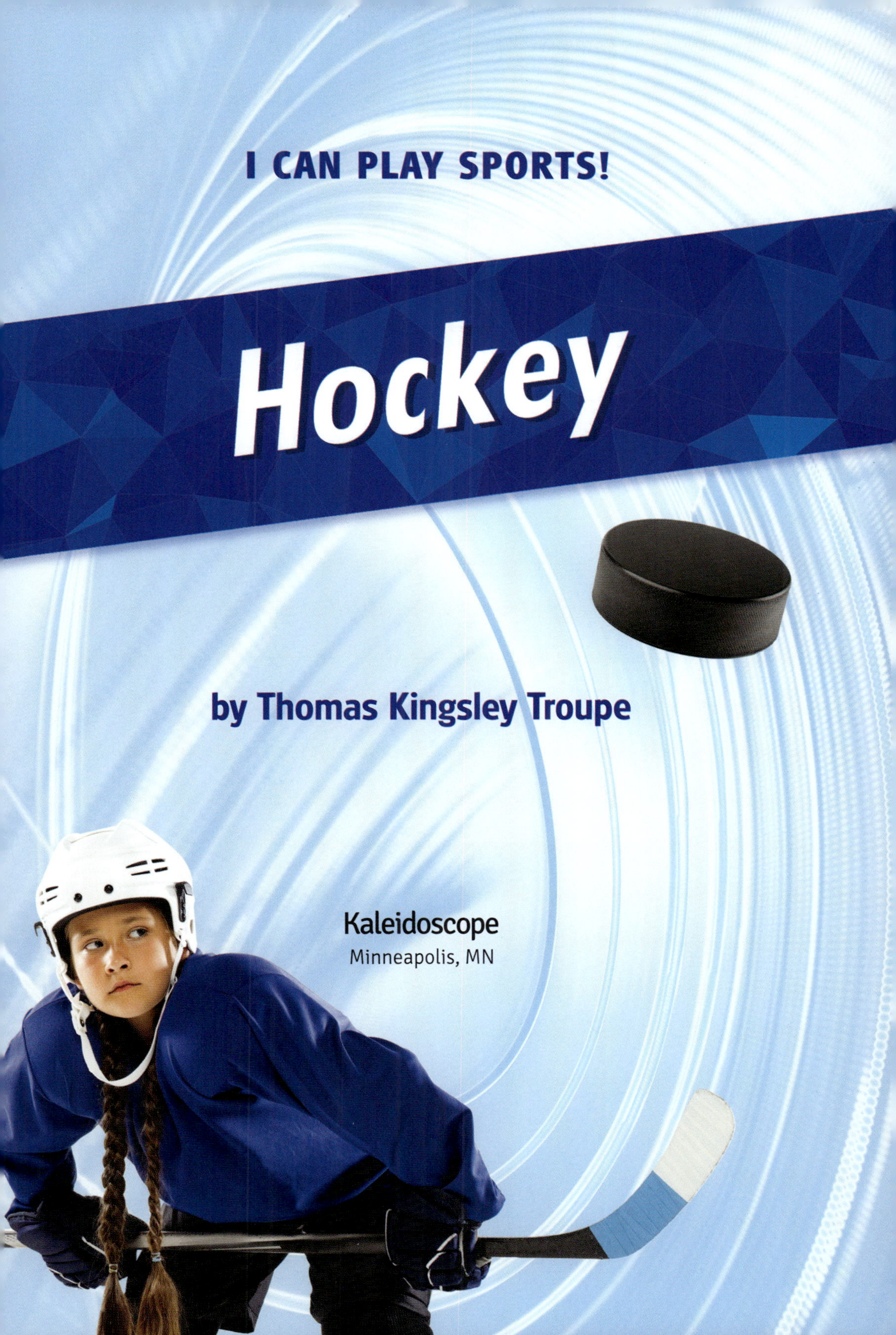

I CAN PLAY SPORTS!

Hockey

by Thomas Kingsley Troupe

Kaleidoscope
Minneapolis, MN

Where the Quest for Discovery Begins

Kaleidoscope Publishing, Inc.
6012 Blue Circle Drive
Minnetonka, MN 55343

Library of Congress Control Number
2022937559

ISBN
978-1-64519-584-9 (library bound)
978-1-64519-654-9 (ebook)

FIND ME IF YOU CAN!

Bigfoot Jr. lurks within one of the images in this book. It's up to you to find him!

Table of Contents

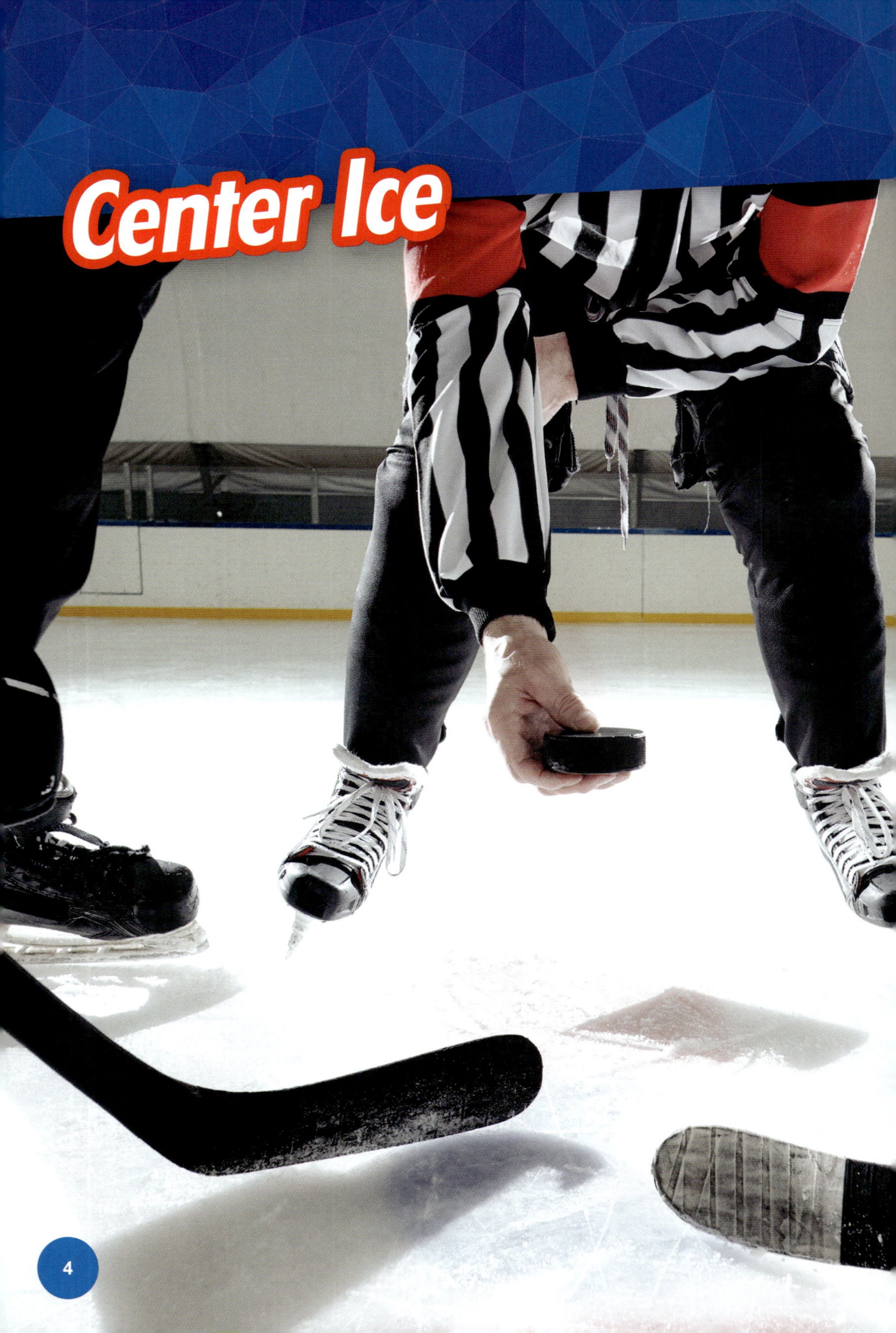

Center Ice

The **referee** drops the **puck**. The hockey game has begun! The players scrap to see who gets the puck.

Players skate to the puck. The **goalie** in the net is ready. A player takes the shot. I can play hockey!

Hockey is played on an ice rink. Games are played outside on an ice rink or inside a **stadium**, or arena.

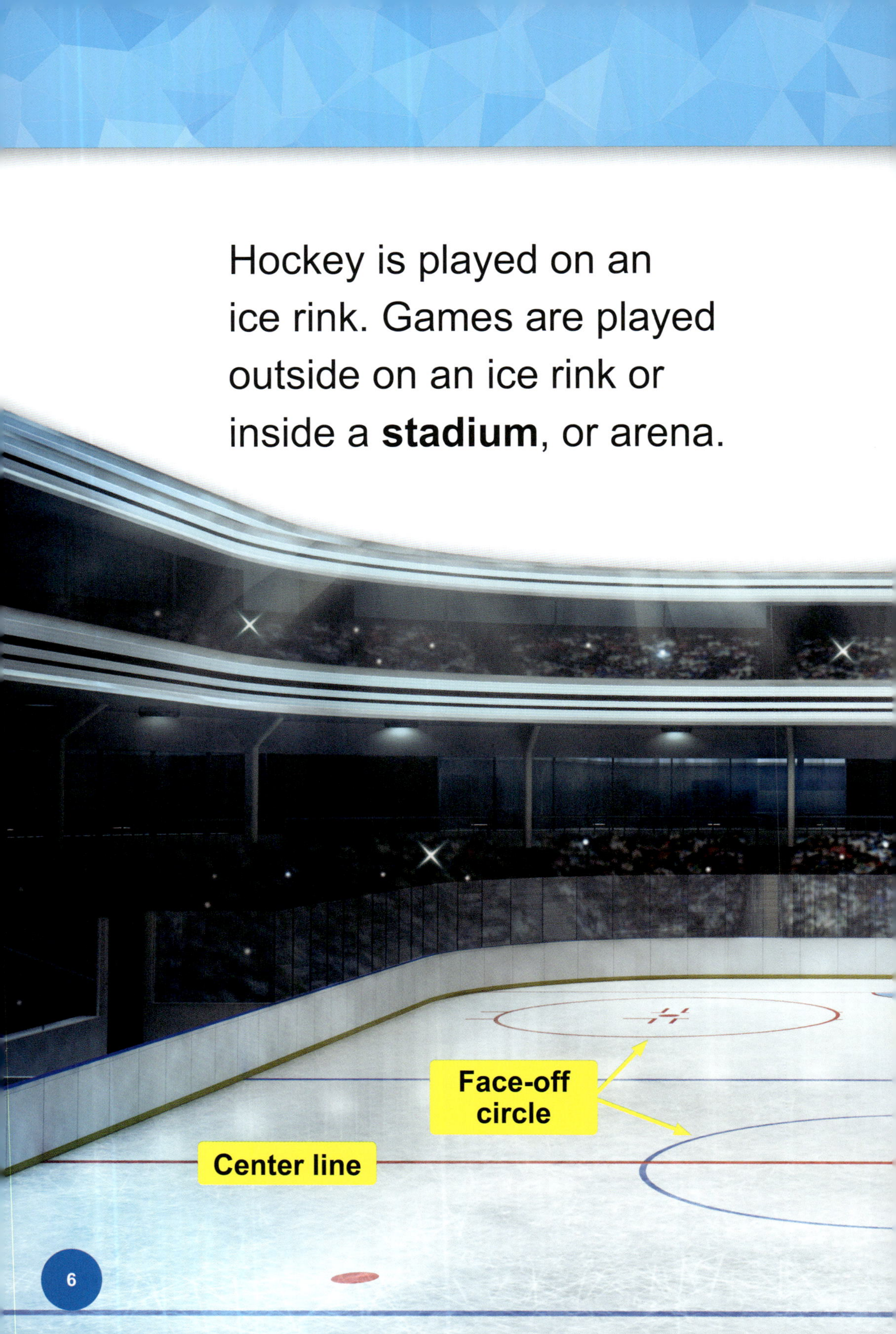

The hockey rink has a goal on each end. There is a net attached to each goal.

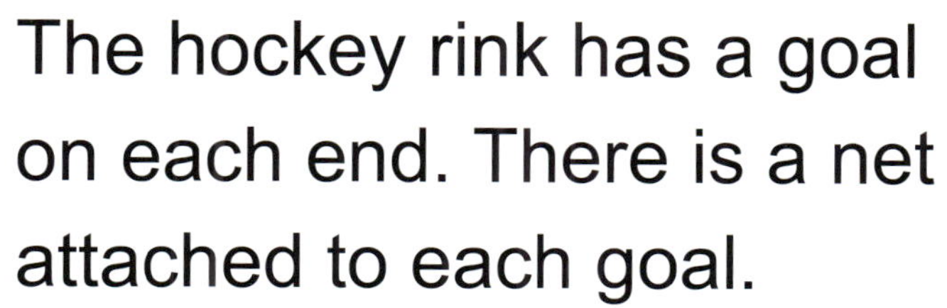

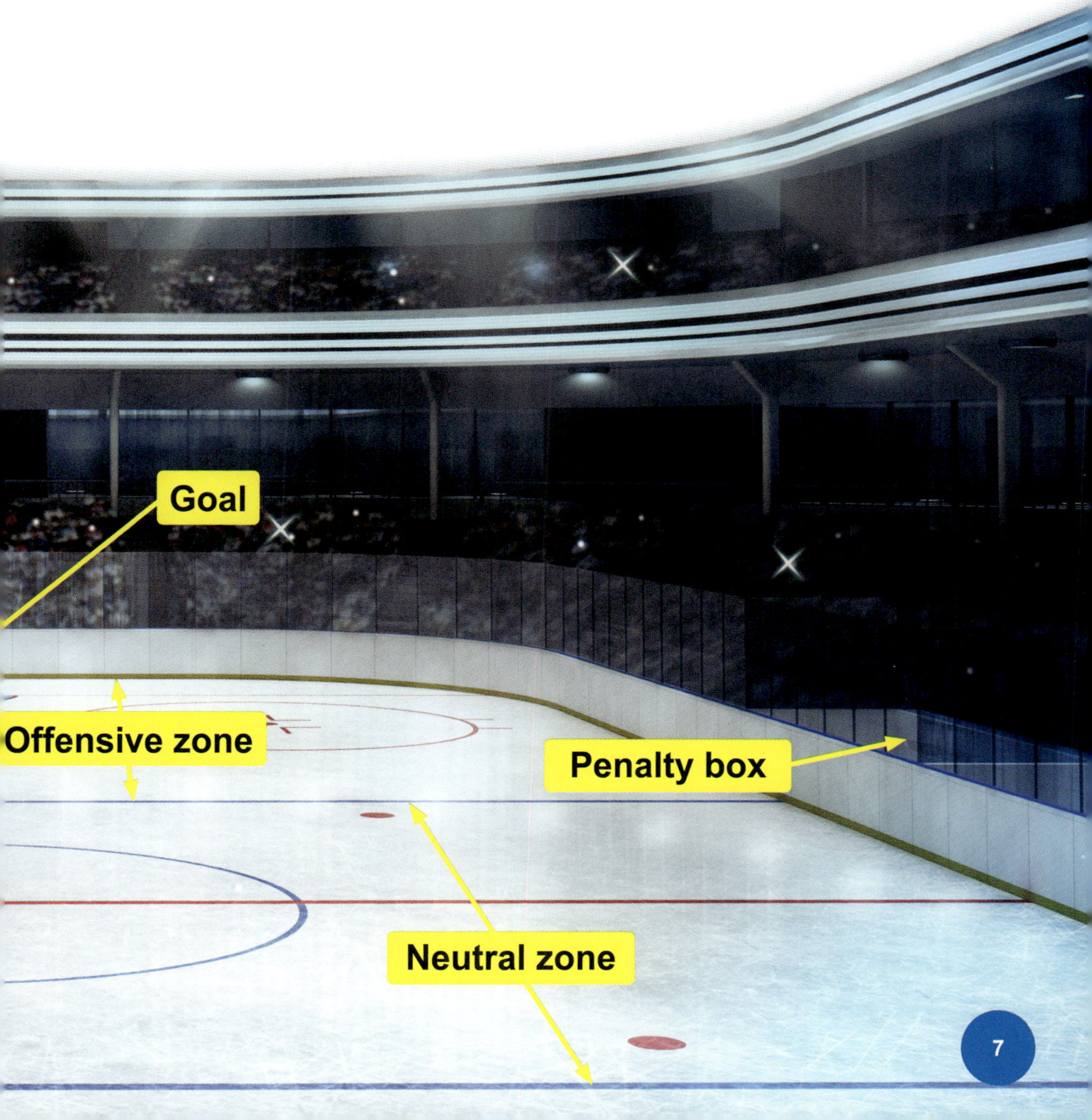

Mouthguard

Players wear helmets on their heads. A **mouthguard** protects their teeth from **injury**.

Players wear pads to keep from getting hurt. They wear skates to move around the rink.

FUN FACT

Hockey was invented in 1875 in Montreal, Canada.

Meet the Team

Each team has six hockey players on the rink. A center plays in the middle.

The center handles **face-offs**. They can move anywhere on the ice and score goals.

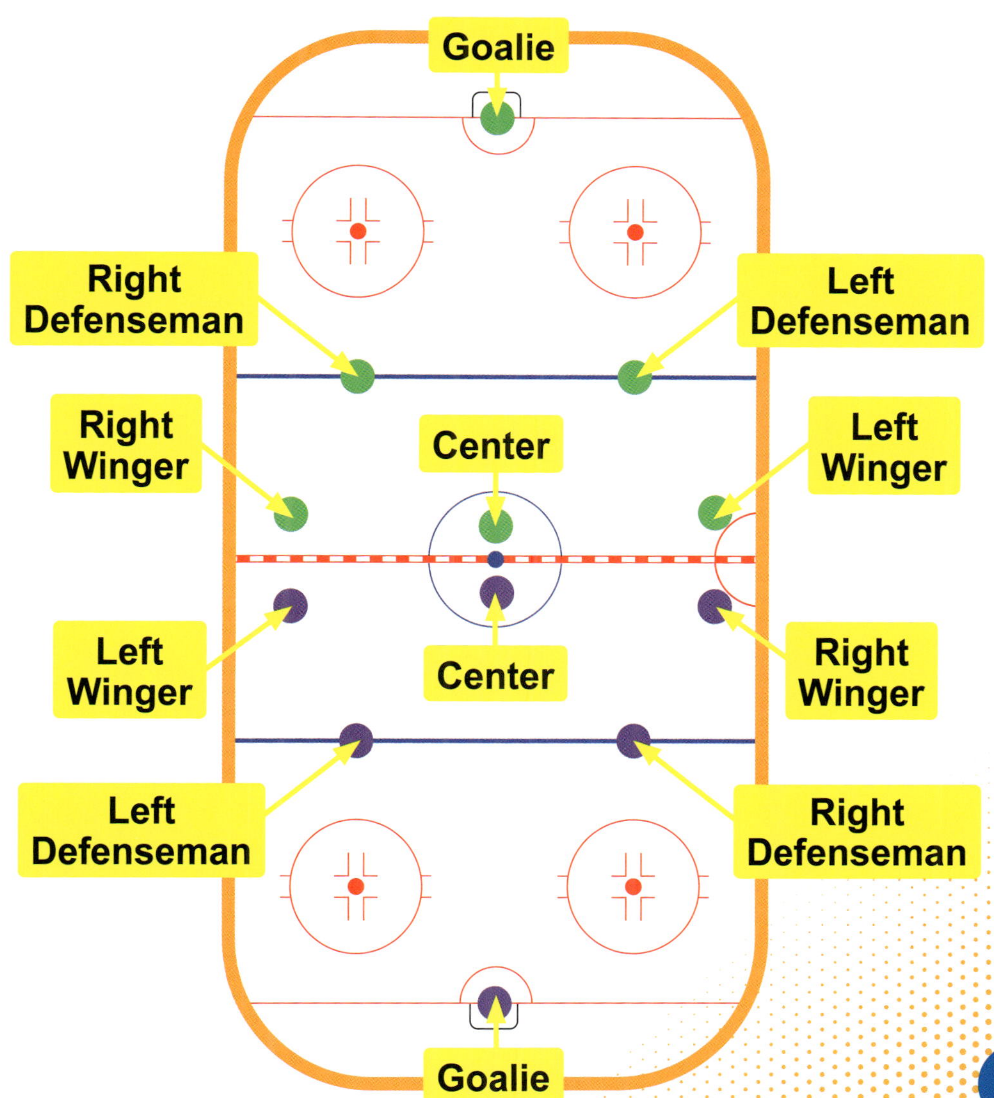

Right and left wings play along the edges of the rink. They try to score goals.

The goalie guards the net. Right and left defenders try to keep the puck away from the net.

FUN FACT

Hockey pro Wayne Gretzky has scored more goals than any other player. His record is 894!

Slap Shot

Hockey sticks move the puck on the ice. Players pass to each other as they skate.

They slap the puck toward the goal. The goalie tries to keep the puck out of the net.

There are five basic skills in hockey

1 Skating
moving around the ice on ice skates

2 Passing
using the stick to pass the puck

3 Stick handling
keeping the puck away from the other team

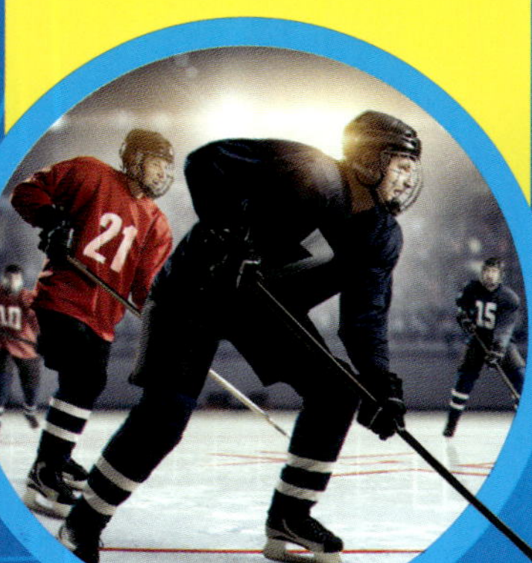

4 Shooting
slapping the puck toward the goal

5 Stopping
coming to a stop on ice skates

A referee blows the whistle if rules are broken. The game will stop for a few moments.

Players who play rough get a time out. They will have to sit in the **penalty** box.

Hat Trick!

Every time the puck enters the goal, the team scores. Usually an alarm sounds.

A goal is worth one point. The team with the most goals by the end wins.

FUN FACT

Goalies wear a lot of pads. An adult goalie's pads weigh around 50 pounds (23 kilograms)!

A scoreboard keeps track of the points scored. It also shows how much time is left in the game.

When the buzzer sounds at the end of the fourth period, the game is over. Both teams had fun.

Photo Glossary

face-offs: When the puck is dropped between two players, the face-off starts the game.

goalie: The player who guards the goal and tries to block the shots.

injury: Any damage to the body that can cause pain or broken bones.

mouthguard: A piece of plastic that players wear to protect their teeth.

penalty: A punishment for breaking a rule in a game. A player can be made to leave the ice and sit in the penalty box.

puck: The rubber disc used in hockey. The puck lands in the net to score.

referee: The sports official who makes sure the rules of the hockey game are followed.

stadium: A large place where fans can watch sporting events.

Read More

Omoth, Tyler. *Hockey Fun.* Mankato, MN, Capstone Publishing, 2021.

Schuh, Mari. *Hockey.* Mankato, MN, Amicus Publishing, 2017.

Sherman, Jill. *Hockey.* Hopkins, MN, Bellwether Media, 2019.

Websites

Factsurfer.com gives you a safe, fun way to find more information.

1. Go to www.factsurfer.com.
2. Enter "Hockey" into the search box and click 🔍
3. Select your book cover to see a list of related websites.

About the Author

Thomas Kingsley Troupe has been reading and writing stories from a very young age. He's the author of over 100 books for kids of all ages. When he's not putting words together, he's fixing his house, watching movies, ghost-hunting or thinking about taking a nap. Thomas lives in Woodbury, MN, with his two ridiculous sons.

INDEX

PHOTO CREDITS

The images in this book are reproduced through the courtesy of: Lucky Business/Shutterstock Images, cover (top); aperturesound/Shutterstock Images, cover, 1 (puck); Anton Vierietin/Shutterstock Images, cover, 1 (girl); Ronnie Chua/Shutterstock Images, p. 3; Pressmaster/Shutterstock Images, p. 4–5, 22 (face-offs); Justaman/Shutterstock Images, p. 5, 22 (goalie); Adam Vilimek/Shutterstock Images, p. 6–7, 22 (stadium); Sergey Novikov/Shutterstock Images, p. 8; Andrii Zhmendak/Shutterstock Images, p. 8, 22 (mouthguard); Sergey Novikov/Shutterstock Images, p. 9 (pads); Shell114/Shutterstock Images, p. 9 (skates); Derek Brumby/Shutterstock Images, p. 9 (Fun Fact); Lucky Business/Shutterstock Images, p. 10; Pikovit/Shutterstock Images, p. 11; Vitalii Vitleo/Shutterstock Images, p. 12; dotshock/Shutterstock Images, p. 13 (top); Luca Santilli/Shutterstock Images, p. 13 (net); Debby Wong/Shutterstock Images, p. 13 (Fun Fact); Irina Boriskina/Shutterstock Images, p. 14–15; Bundit Yuwannasiri/Shutterstock Images, p. 15 (Fun Fact); Domenic Gareri/Shutterstock Images, p. 16 (shooting); Lorraine Swanson/Shutterstock Images, p. 16 (stopping); Sergey Nivens/Shutterstock Images, p. 16 (stick handling); Sergey Novikov/Shutterstock Images, p. 16 (passing); Master1305/Shutterstock Images, p. 16 (skating); Olga Pinegina/Shutterstock Images, p. 17 (referee); DardaInna/Shutterstock Images, p. 17; Click Images/Shutterstock Images, p. 18; VanoVasaio/Shutterstock Images, p. 19; Michael Pettigrew/Shutterstock Images, p. 19 (Fun Fact); Emmoth/Shutterstock Images, p. 20; Lucky Business/Shutterstock Images, p. 21 (top); Lucky Business/Shutterstock Images, p. 21 (circle); Vaclav Volrab/Shutterstock Images, p. 22 (puck); Shooter Bob Square Lenses/Shutterstock Images, p. 22 (referee); dotshock/Shutterstock Images, p. 22 (penalty); Paul Yates/Shutterstock Images, p. 22 (injury); Andrey_Popov/Shutterstock Images, p. 23.